CLOSER LOOK AT

EARTHQUAKES

Joyce Pope

Franklin Watts
LONDON ● SYDNEY

An Aladdin Book
© Aladdin Books Ltd 1996
Designed and produced by
Aladdin Books Ltd
28 Percy Street
London W1P 0LD

*First published in Great Britain
in 1996 by*
Franklin Watts
96 Leonard Street
London EC2A 4RH

ISBN: 0 7496 2471 X

CIP data for this book is available from
the British Library

Editor
Alex Edmonds

Designer
Gary Edgar-Hyde

Picture Research
Brooks Krikler Research

Front cover illustration
Gary Edgar-Hyde

Illustrators
Ian Moores
Mike Saunders
Gary Edgar-Hyde

Certain illustrations have appeared in
earlier books created by Aladdin Books.

Consultant
Cally Hall BSc (Hons) is a geologist. She is a museum
gemmologist. She is also a fellow of the Gemmological
Association of Great Britain. Cally is an author, editor and
consultant, and has appeared on television and given radio
interviews.

Printed in Belgium

CONTENTS

INTRODUCTION

During an earthquake, the power of the planet shows itself. Rocks deep in the Earth's crust shift and tear, causing devastation to towns and countryside alike. After the quake the change in the surface rocks usually seems slight, but there may well be immense damage to humans and their environment. Over large areas, houses may have been flattened, huge buildings may have fallen, and roads and bridges may be cracked and impassable.

An earthquake strikes without warning. Suddenly, everything that you thought was solid and strong changes. Your house shudders. Run outside and you will see the ground rolling, like waves over the sea. As houses and office blocks collapse, power lines may be brought down and gas mains broken, so fire often adds to the general confusion.

The tragedy
These women (above) are survivors of a quake that left 30,000 dead in northern India in 1993. Their homes are flattened and they have lost all they own, and possibly family members. The effect of the quake will be lifelong for them.

CAUGHT IN

THE WORLD TEARS OPEN

In most years there are about 500,000 earthquakes. The majority of these are very small and can only be noticed by very sensitive machines. About 1,000 of them cause some damage, and in most years at least one earthquake is a major catastrophe, such as this earthquake in California (left). Although an earthquake usually starts deep below the ground, it forces the rocks at the surface to form into waves. Most rocks are too fragile for this treatment, so they split apart. Sometimes openings appear and close again. Often, as in this picture (right), surface rocks break and shift, leaving cracks that may be big enough for cars, or even whole houses, to fall into.

ON CLOSER INSPECTION
– The effect

If you are indoors during an earthquake, the room sways like a ship. You can get an idea of what it is like to be in a small earthquake if you stand by a road as a big lorry thunders past. The ground shudders, but the moment passes without serious damage.

AN EARTHQUAKE

HOW LONG DO THEY LAST?

Tension in the Earth's crust may build up for hundreds of years, as at the San Andreas Fault in California (below). When it reaches breaking point the earthquake takes only a few minutes. Often it lasts for ten seconds or less. If it is big, there may be brief aftershocks.

The San Andreas Fault

The huge San Andreas Fault system stretches for over 1,210 kilometres, following the coast of California in the USA. Today it is easy to see the dramatic evidence of the fault in cracked walls and scarred landscapes like the one below.

E arthquakes may happen on land or under the sea. They are rarest in areas of ancient rock that lie at the very centre of the continents. They are common at the edges of the great tectonic plates (see p.9) that fit together like a jigsaw over the Earth's surface. The plates push against each other under pressure, and this causes the earthquake.

WHERE DO

San Andreas Fault

San Francisco

FAULTS

When great areas of the Earth's crust push against each other, the rocks bend and sometimes break under the strain. These breaks are called faults. Presently some places are under constant pressure and faults are still moving, like the San Andreas Fault system in California (see above and right).

Major fault

Daly City

The Pacific Plate is slowly moving north-west at 5-6 cm per year. Scraping this and the North American Fault has caused other smaller faults.

Parkfield

Bakersfield

On Closer Inspection
– *Earthquakes too*

When a volcano erupts there are usually earthquakes at the same time. The Ring of Fire (land at the edge of the Pacific Ocean, where the most volcanoes occur) is also an earthquake zone. Mount St Helens (right), which erupted in 1980, is in the Ring of Fire.

THEY HAPPEN?

San Andreas Fault

Epicentre

Pacific Plate

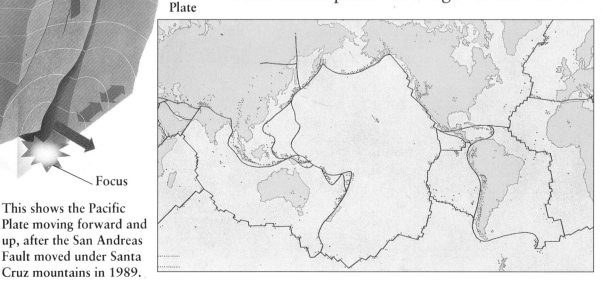

North American Plate

Focus

Los Angeles

This shows the Pacific Plate moving forward and up, after the San Andreas Fault moved under Santa Cruz mountains in 1989.

THE EARTH'S PLATES

The Earth's surface is not continuous, but is divided into great sections called tectonic plates, which carry the continents and the ocean bed. There are a number of large plates that are named, and several smaller ones. They move about slowly, shifting at most a few centimetres a year. Volcanoes and earthquakes occur where plates move against each other.

The build-up to the quake

Before the main quake starts, instruments may record a brief tremor. This is called the foreshock. It is caused by the first movement as rocks, stressed to breaking point, begin to fracture. After the main movement, there may be slight adjustments as the rocks finally settle into a new position. These give what are known as aftershocks.

An earthquake starts when rocks in the Earth's crust or mantle tear and slip into a new position. The point at which this happens is called the focus of the earthquake. Waves of energy spread in all directions from the focus. The first point at which they reach the surface is called the epicentre. This is the place where the greatest damage occurs.

HOW DO

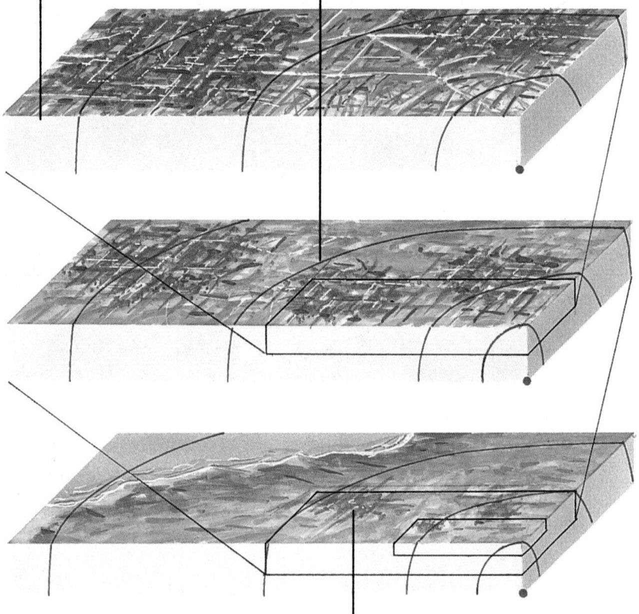

1. 70 km deep. Focus causes shock waves over small area.

2. 70-300 km deep. Focus causes shock waves over larger area.

3. 300 km deep. Focus causes shock waves over huge areas.

This diagram shows how the depth of focus of an earthquake affects how far the shock waves travel, causing damage over a wide area.

THE FOCUS

During an earthquake, in which two plates push into each other, or grind past one another, the focus of the quake is shallow, in the rocks of the crust. Deep-focus earthquakes are caused by one plate riding over the other, pushing it far down into the Earth's mantle. The deeper the focus of an earthquake, the further the waves will pass through the Earth (see left). The focus of the quake can be calculated by finding out how strong the waves are and which direction they have come from.

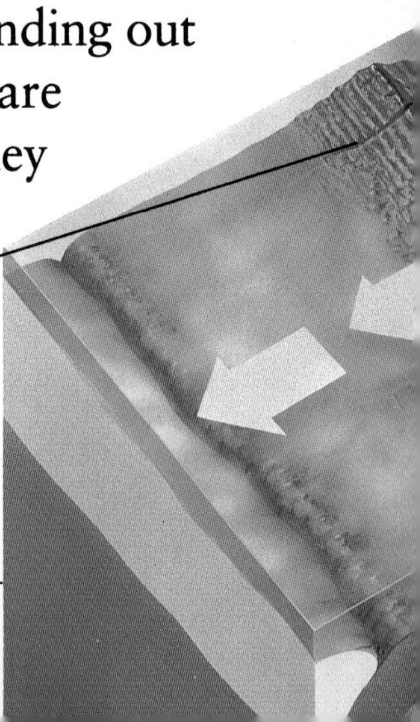

Oceanic ridge

At an oceanic ridge, hot, molten rock rises and creates strain in the rocks until it is relieved by an earthquake, which will usually be small.

ON CLOSER INSPECTION
– *History unravelled*

Old rocks can show us where earthquakes once took place. We can see folded rocks that were squeezed up into folds. Sometimes they broke and slipped. Geologists call breaks and slips like this "faults". The faults in this cliff tell of ancient stresses and earthquakes.

THEY START?

In a subduction zone, new ocean floor is pulled back into the mantle. This causes heat and strain which produce deep-focus earthquakes.

When two plates grind against each other along a transform fault, the pressure causes the rocks to snap, causing shock waves below the surface.

Fold mountains

Plates

Subduction zone

When two plates crash into each other, the rock slips, creating mountains, or it folds up, causing shallow-focus earthquakes.

Shallow-focus earthquake

Transform fault

Deep-focus earthquake

Rising magma

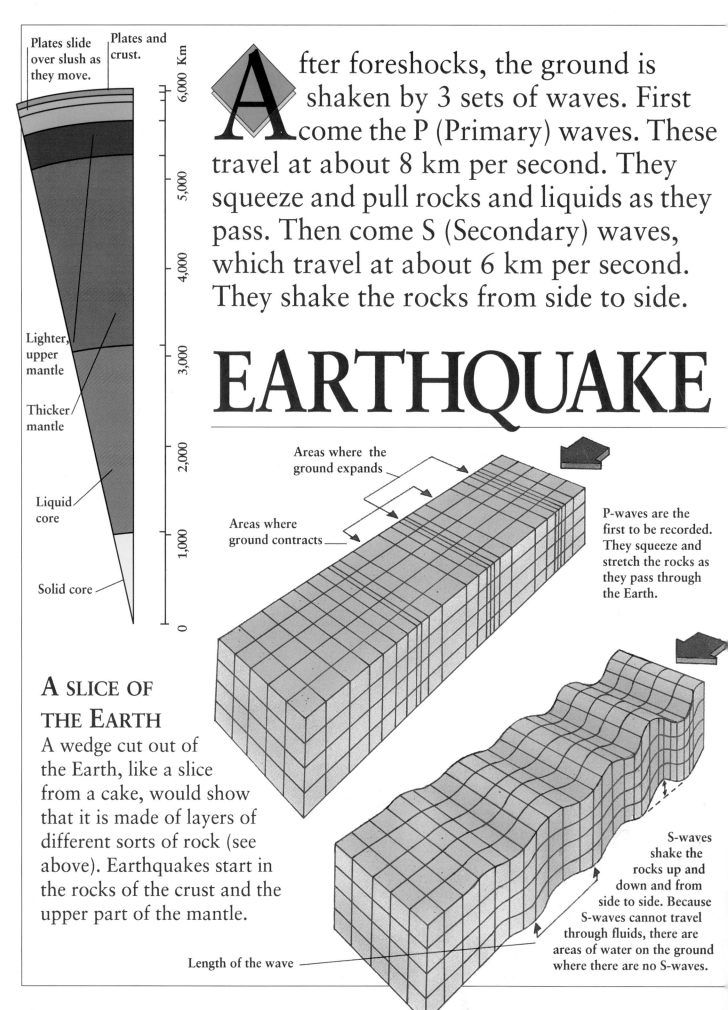

Plates slide over slush as they move.

Plates and crust.

6,000 Km

5,000

4,000

Lighter, upper mantle

3,000

Thicker mantle

2,000

Liquid core

1,000

Solid core

0

After foreshocks, the ground is shaken by 3 sets of waves. First come the P (Primary) waves. These travel at about 8 km per second. They squeeze and pull rocks and liquids as they pass. Then come S (Secondary) waves, which travel at about 6 km per second. They shake the rocks from side to side.

EARTHQUAKE

Areas where the ground expands

Areas where ground contracts

P-waves are the first to be recorded. They squeeze and stretch the rocks as they pass through the Earth.

A SLICE OF THE EARTH

A wedge cut out of the Earth, like a slice from a cake, would show that it is made of layers of different sorts of rock (see above). Earthquakes start in the rocks of the crust and the upper part of the mantle.

S-waves shake the rocks up and down and from side to side. Because S-waves cannot travel through fluids, there are areas of water on the ground where there are no S-waves.

Length of the wave

On Closer Inspection
– Hidden faults?

The fault, or fracture, that causes these earthquakes is usually deep within the Earth. In some cases it is visible at the surface – for example, at the San Andreas Fault. Faults like this usually produce shallow earthquakes.

WAVES

THE MOST LETHAL WAVES

The last of the earthquake waves to be felt are called L-waves. They travel more slowly than the others, at not more than about 4 km per second. In spite of this they cause the most damage, for they are only felt on the surface of the Earth.

L-waves make the ground roll beneath your feet. They open chasms in the rocks and shake down buildings.

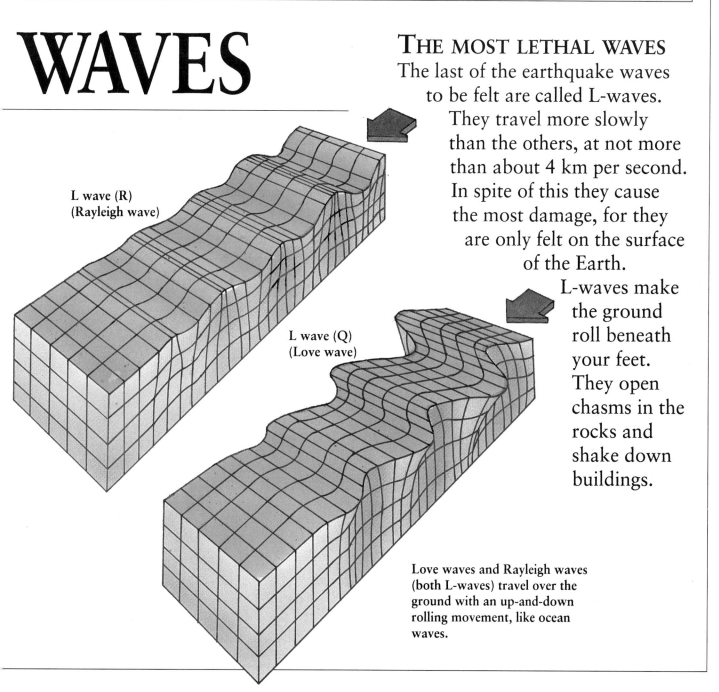

L wave (R)
(Rayleigh wave)

L wave (Q)
(Love wave)

Love waves and Rayleigh waves (both L-waves) travel over the ground with an up-and-down rolling movement, like ocean waves.

Wet and wild

Tsunamis often cause more damage than the actual earth tremor. They may flood towns and drown thousands of people. One of the biggest this century threw waves 530 metres on to the land. Sometimes, as below, the force of the tsunami causes large boats to be stranded far from the sea and general devastation.

Most of the Earth's surface is covered by oceans, and many earthquakes occur under the water. This may be where plates are growing, or where faulting occurs for other reasons. The focus of underwater quakes can be pinpointed, and changes in the sea bed can be charted by ships with sensitive depth sounders.

EARTHQUAKES

When the tsunami nears the shore, its waves become closer together, and taller.

The tsunami pounds down on the coast and surges inland. It sweeps away everything in its path.

UNDER THE SEA

TIDAL WAVE!

Although earthquakes under the sea do not affect the land directly, the sudden change in the sea bed can cause tsunamis to be formed. In the open ocean tsunamis are not great – usually not more than a metre high. There may be more than 100 km between one crest and the next. But they travel fast, often at over 700 km per hour. As a tsunami approaches land where there are shelving beaches and narrow inlets, the water towers into a huge wave, which does tremendous damage when it crashes ashore.

The waves make the sea floor jolt, which creates large sea waves.

When an earthquake occurs below the ocean floor, part of the sea bed is forced up.

House problems
Damage caused by earthquakes (above) is often made greater by fires caused by gas or oil leaking. Huge sums of money are needed to repair the damage caused by earthquakes.

he destructive powers of earthquakes are felt most strongly where cities are built on soft rocks such as sands and silts, because L-waves can pass through these most easily. But loss of life and damage to property tend to be greatest where houses and other buildings are made of stone.

THE POWER

1,000 ATOMIC BOMBS

It is difficult to imagine the power of an earthquake. Atomic bombs are the only human inventions that can compare with forces able to move thousands of tonnes of rocks in a few seconds. Even so, the energy released by a single atomic bomb could cause only a small earthquake. It has been calculated that an earthquake in Mexico in 1985 was about equal to 1,000 atomic bombs as large as the one that destroyed the city of Hiroshima in 1945.

The force of an earthquake shatters walls and destroys homes (left).

The ancient Greeks believed that a great bull lived in tunnels below the palace of Knossos, in Crete. His bellowing was thought to shake the Earth. This is perhaps how the Greeks explained what happened in an earthquake.

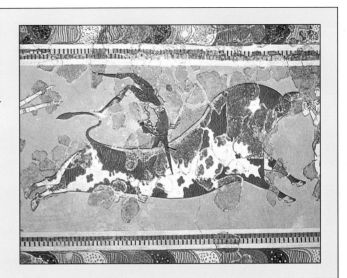

OF EARTHQUAKES

COMMUNICATION PROBLEMS

After an earthquake, rescue can be difficult if entry to the area is hard. The destruction of roads, bridges and tunnels adds to the chaos caused by earthquakes, as seen left, in the 1995 earthquake at Kobe, Japan. Some bad earthquakes have been in mountainous areas. This has made rescuing victims even harder than usual.

SAN FRANCISCO – 1989

An earthquake may cause damage over a large area. The earthquake in 1989 in San Francisco, USA, affected a million km^2 of land. In the city itself damage to buildings and roads was estimated at $6,000 million (right). Sixty-three people were killed and 4,000 injured.

Scientists can tell the strength of a quake using the Richter Scale. This is based on the energy released in an earthquake shock, calculated from seismograph readings. The largest Richter number of any recent earthquake was 8.9 (over 7 is considered to be a major earthquake), recorded in the Chilean earthquake of 1960.

Seismographs

A seismograph reading (below) shows the time at which an earthquake takes place, and how long it lasts. The more jagged the line, the greater the shock. The reading from a big quake will show three different periods of shaking, produced by the P-, S- and L-waves.

MEASURING

MERCALLI SCALE

The Mercalli Scale was first invented in 1902, and modified in 1931, so that it now applies to damage in modern cities. It runs from strength 1, which is a quake felt by very few people, to strength 12, which can totally destroy whole towns and kill all of the inhabitants.

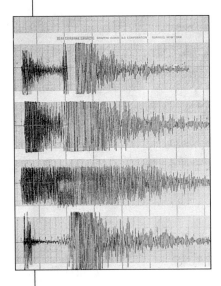

3. Similar to a large passing vehicle.

4. Felt by many people indoors.

1. Felt by only some people.

2. Felt by a few, on upper floors.

ON CLOSER INSPECTION
– *Seismographs*

A sensitive spring and a weight are attached to a rigid frame. The frame moves when the ground shakes. A pen records the movement as a line on a rotating drum. Seismographs record vertical and side-to-side movements in the Earth's crust.

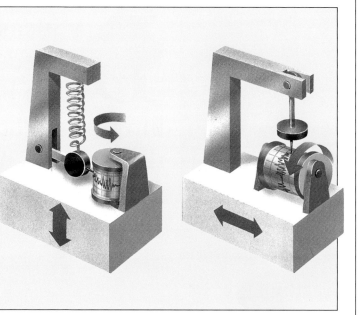

AN EARTHQUAKE

5. Buildings tremble and trees shake.

7. Bricks loosen. Difficult to stand.

9. Pipes crack. Buildings collapse.

6. Felt by everyone. Plaster cracks.

8. Damage to weak structures.

10. Huge ground cracks. Landslides

11. Most buildings destroyed. Tsunamis form.

12. Total destruction. Surface waves in ground visible.

By measuring the direction and speeds of P- and S-waves, scientists have been able to explore the interior of the Earth. P- and S-waves pass through the mantle at high speeds, but at a depth of about 3,000 km below the surface, they meet the Earth's outer core and the S-waves can go no further.

Earthquake zone

At a depth of about 35 km from the surface of an earthquake zone (above), the speed of P- and S-waves changes. Geologists have tried to drill down to reach this point, where the interior of the Earth really begins.

S-WAVES

The S-waves stop, because the Earth's outer core is made of melted rocks. The side-to-side S-waves cannot pass through liquids. P-waves can. They also pass through the solid core, but the waves change direction slightly when they reach the liquid outer core. They emerge into the mantle and the plates on the surface of the far side of the world.

WHAT QUAKES

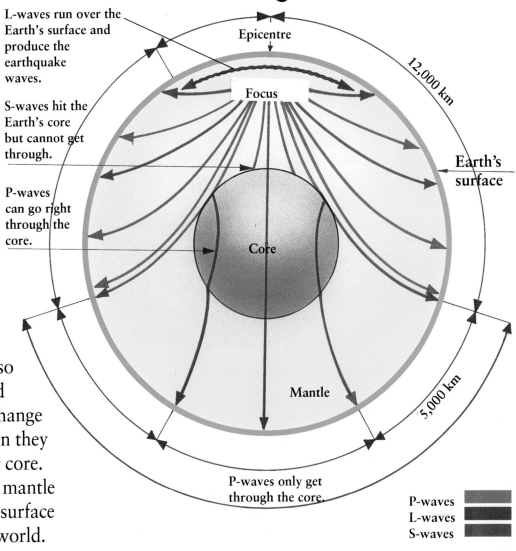

L-waves run over the Earth's surface and produce the earthquake waves.

S-waves hit the Earth's core but cannot get through.

P-waves can go right through the core.

Epicentre

Focus

12,000 km

Earth's surface

Core

Mantle

5,000 km

P-waves only get through the core.

P-waves
L-waves
S-waves

ON CLOSER INSPECTION
– Explosive work

Geologists may need to explore and map the rocks below the Earth's surface. They often mimic earthquakes by making explosions below ground. This work tells geologists where rocks bearing oil or minerals occur.

HAVE TAUGHT US

MAN-MADE EARTHQUAKES

Human beings can cause earthquakes too. Often they are produced when a dam has been built, such as the Hoover Dam (below), holding up millions of tonnes of incredibly heavy water. The rocks below the dam have been stressed and shifted, like those at the edges of plates. This tension then results in earthquakes.

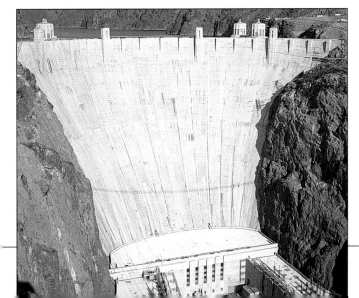

DAM DISASTERS

The Kariba Dam in Africa (above), holds back the world's largest artificial lake. It is a major project which disrupts rocks below the Earth's surface. Another example is the Boulder Dam in Arizona. In the years after it had been built, 6,000 minor earthquakes were recorded.

Port Royal

In 1692 a great earthquake destroyed Port Royal in Jamaica (below). Twenty thousand people were killed in the earthquake. Port Royal was an important pirate centre for the West Indies, and had traded in slaves and rum. Because of this, many people believed that the earthquake was God's way of punishing the town.

In many parts of the world, throughout all human history, earthquakes have brought terror to city dwellers. Ephesus and many other beautiful ancient cities of what is now southern Turkey, have been wrecked by earthquakes. Even remains in South America, of Mayan and Inca civilisations, show earthquake damage as far back as the 4th century BC.

EARTHQUAKES

LISBON EARTHQUAKE

In Portugal, in November 1755, shock waves from the first tremors of what was to be a devastating earthquake travelled from the epicentre to the city of Lisbon in seconds. As the earthquake shook the city, people rushed into the open, but many were killed by collapsing buildings. Fire followed, then huge tsunamis raced in from the ocean and swept across all but the highest part of the town. About 60,000 people were killed in Lisbon, and others died in nearby Spain and North Africa.

ON CLOSER INSPECTION
– *Chinese quake sensor*

A tremor causes a weight inside a pot to swing. This causes one of the dragons on the outside of the pot to open its mouth and drop a bronze ball. Metal toads with open mouths surround the pot to catch the falling balls. The toad that is the farthest away from the epicentre catches the ball first.

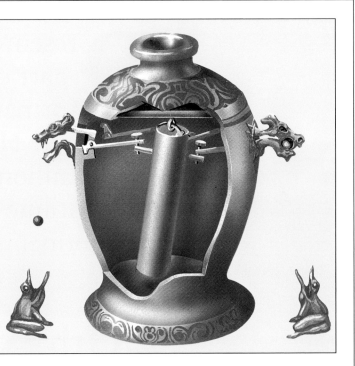

IN HISTORY

From the banks of the River Tagus, a 24 kilometre wave hurled itself across the city.

Fire spread through the city and burned for nearly 3 days, destroying everything.

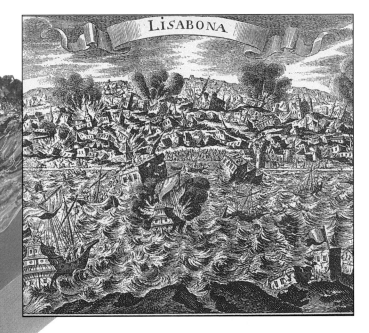

Lisbon ruins
This woodcut depicts the general devastation caused by the 1755 earthquake. It shows the effects of the tsunamis which not only destroyed homes and towns but also tore apart ships and boats on the ocean.

P̲resent-day earthquakes are part of the final phases of the formation of great mountains such as the Himalayas. Although this began millions of years ago, earthquakes still continue as the plates that carry the continents push into each other.

20th-CENTURY

Turkey
Turkey (above) and the countries of western Asia have been the site of many great earthquakes in the past. This is because the Turkish Plate is being pushed by two other plates, like the blades of a pair of scissors. By looking at the history of the quakes, scientists have learned how the plate is moving.

Scientists use modern camera techniques to construct how it would appear if you were in a serious earthquake (right).

CALIFORNIAN EARTHQUAKES
In 1906 an earthquake measuring about 7.8 on the Richter scale struck San Francisco, killing over 700 people. In 1989 another, measuring 7.1, caused huge damage when a concrete highway collapsed. Los Angeles has also suffered from powerful quakes. The San Andreas and other faults run near to both cities.

ON CLOSER INSPECTION
– *Rescue dogs*

When an earthquake strikes, homeless people need shelter, blankets and food. Trained sniffer dogs are sometimes sent to detect survivors buried under rubble.

EARTHQUAKES

INDIA

Northern India (below), Pakistan and Afghanistan have all suffered in recent years from earthquakes registering between 6.8 and 7.0 on the Richter Scale. Because these quakes have taken place in remote regions, few people have been killed.

JAPAN

The crowded cities of Japan have suffered more from earthquakes than any other part of the world. The most recent serious quake was in 1995 (above), when a quake killed over 5,000 people and injured over 25,000 in Kobe. This was caused by a fault that had not shifted for 1,000 years and was thought to be safe.

To predict an earthquake, scientists need to discover where and how fast rocks are moving along geological faults. Seismologists have discovered several warning signs in the build up of an earthquake – such as changes in seismic waves and lots of minor tremors along plate edges. Using modern technology along with these signals, they try and predict earthquakes.

The race is on
Scientists in Japan (above) study computers for signs of earthquake activity. Laser beams can also be reflected across fault lines to show tiny ground movements. The beams are sent from specially-made huts (right).

PREDICTING

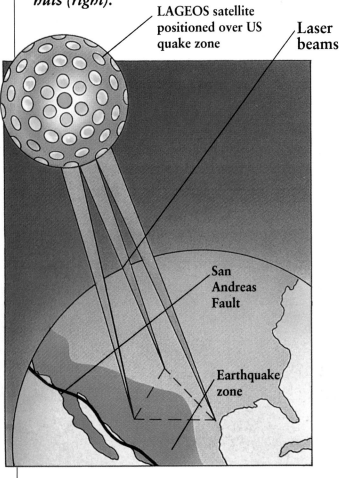

LAGEOS satellite positioned over US quake zone

Laser beams

San Andreas Fault

Earthquake zone

BE PREPARED
In California they expect an earthquake measuring 6.7 on the Richter Scale every 11 years. But during the last 195 years there have been far fewer than this, so it looks as if the rocks sliding past each other in the faults are stuck. Scientists say they will soon move, causing an earthquake – but they don't know when.

On Closer Inspection
– Animal problems

In parts of the world without scientific equipment, people watch animal behaviour to give them a clue about earthquakes that are on the way. Many animals, such as horses, show signs of distress. They are probably reacting to small foreshocks that humans cannot feel.

EARTHQUAKES

STRAIN METER

The white, bin-like object protects a hole containing a strain meter (below). This records the amount of water underground and in the rocks, which alters with the pressure of seismic movements on the rocks. Solar panels power the equipment.

CREEP METER

A creep meter (above) measures rock movements along a fault. If water is pumped into moving fault areas it acts as a lubricant. The rocks move smoothly against each other and so cause only small ground tremors.

People living in earthquake zones have to be prepared for the worst. Tokyo in Japan, one of the most quake-struck cities in the world, monitors fault movements constantly to warn of large quakes. There are trained disaster teams ready to go to work in an emergency, and food and blankets and huge supplies of water for fighting fires are held in readiness.

PREPARING

BEING PREPARED

The TransAmerica building in San Francisco (left) stands 255 metres high. It is built to withstand even the most severe earthquake. Its triangular frame is supported by concrete-covered steel columns to give it the necessary strength.

Schoolchildren in Japan practise their earthquake drills (right).

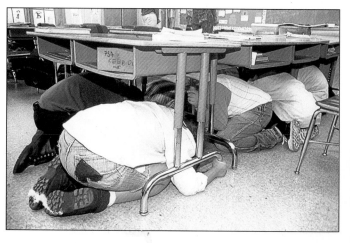

ON CLOSER INSPECTION
– *Street safety*

Simple precautions can help reduce earthquake damage. Wide, straight streets, like these in San Francisco, can help to prevent the spread of fire. Wide streets also leave space between the rubble of fallen buildings for the emergency services to rescue people.

FOR EARTHQUAKES

Chimneys are secured with special brackets.

Beams and joists are reinforced.

A SAFE HOME

There are now known ways to make houses safer. They should be low, with strengthened foundations and upper walls, and beams firmly fixed to withstand the swaying L-waves that cause most of the damage. Some of the more bizarre-looking designs include this San Franciscan home (above).

Foundations are reinforced with steel rods. Walls are secured to the foundations.

Water heaters, boilers etc. are secured to prevent them breaking loose and cracking gas pipes.

A fault in the ground in San Francisco, USA.

EARTHQUAKE INVENTORY

Year	Place	Richter Scale No.	Number of casualties
1201	Eastern Mediterranean		1.1 million dead
1692	Port Royal, Jamaica		more than 2,000 dead
1755	Lisbon, Portugal		more than 60,000 dead
1873	Southern Italy		51,000 dead
1906	Colombia/Ecuador	8.6	
1906	Valparaiso, Chile	8.4	
1906	San Francisco, USA	7.8	

Clearing up after the 1991 quake in Georgia.

Year	Place	Richter Scale No.	Number of casualties
1911	Sinkiang, China	–	
1920	Kansu, China	–	
1923	Sagami Bay, Tokyo	8.2	
1933	Japanese Trench	8.5	
1955	North Assam, India	8.6	
1960	Chile	8.9	
1964	Alaska	8.6	few killed, more than $750 million damage
1976	Tangshan, China	7.9	242,000 dead
1985	Mexico City, Mexico	8.1	
1988	Armenia	6.9	25,000 dead

The aftermath of the 1991 quake in northern India.

Year	Place	Richter Scale No.	Number of casualties
1989	San Francisco, USA	6.9	63 dead
1990	Iran	7.7	35,000 dead
1990	Peru	5.8	more than 100 dead
1990	Romania	6.5-7.0	about 70 dead
1990	Philippines	7.7	over 1,500 dead
1991	Northern India	7.1	500 dead
1991	Hindu Kush, Afghanistan	6.5-6.8	1,000 dead
1991	Central America	7.5	more than 80 dead
1991	Georgia	7.2	more than 100 dead
1995	Kobe, Japan	6.9-70	5,000 dead

Aftershocks Vibrations caused by the movement of rocks as they settle into their new position after an earthquake.

Crust The outermost layer of the Earth, consisting of rocks that form the land and ocean floor.

Epicentre The point on the Earth's surface immediately above the focus of an earthquake.

Fault A crack in the rocks that form the Earth's surface. Blocks of rock separated by faults may move vertically or sideways.

Focus The point where the rocks start pushing or grinding against one another, producing an earthquake.

Fold A bend in layers of rock caused by plate movements.

Lava Molten rock that pours from a volcano.

Magma Molten rock that lies below the Earth's crust in the mantle.

Mantle The layer of the Earth between the crust and the outer core.

Oceanic ridges These occur down the middle of the major oceans where the crustal plates are moving apart. Molten rock from beneath the crust constantly wells up between the two plates. The ridges are formed from the cooling lava creating new ocean floor.

Richter Scale A scale measuring the strength of an earthquake by using

information from a seismograph.

Seismograph An instrument for measuring the time, size and direction of an earthquake.

Seismologist A scientist who studies earthquakes.

Subduction zone A place where the ocean floor is submerging into the mantle beneath another plate. The heat from the mantle causes the rock to melt.

GLOSSARY

Tectonic plate One of the large slabs of rock that form the Earth's crust. The plates move very slowly as they float on the molten magma beneath them. Continental plates are five or six times thicker than oceanic plates.

Tremor Also called a foreshock, this is a vibration of the ground caused by the first movement as stressed rocks begin to break.

Tsunami A large sea wave caused by an earthquake or volcanic eruption, which often does tremendous damage to coastal regions.

Volcano A rift or vent in the Earth's crust through which molten rock erupts from deep within the Earth and flows over the surface.

INDEX